Imaginarium

Also by the same author

Poetry

A Few Questions About Paradise (Loonfeather Press)

Translation

The Forest: Poems by Besnik Mustafaj (PM Chapbooks)

Imaginarium

Poems by

Lynn Levin

Loonfeather Press
Bemidji, Minnesota

Cover Design: Bill Donnelly/WT Design
Cover Art © Photothèque des Musées de la Ville de Paris: *Peace Comes to Console Men and Restore Abundance* or *The Disconsolate Earth Lifting Her Eyes to Heaven to Secure an End to Her Misfortunes/La paix vient consoler les hommes et ramène l'abondance*, 1849/1854 by Eugène Delacroix.

Photograph of Painting: Pierrain
Author's Photograph: David Graham
Book Design: Betty Rossi

First Printing: 2005
Printed in Canada
ISBN 0-926147-18-8

Imaginarium is printed on 100 percent recycled material including 20 percent post-consumer waste. This acid-free paper is oxygen-bleached, an environmentally friendly process.

Loonfeather Press is a not-for-profit small press organized under section 501 (c) (3) of the United States Internal Revenue Code.

Loonfeather Press
P.O. Box 1212
Bemidji, MN 56619

ACKNOWLEDGMENTS

Grateful acknowledgment goes to the following publications in which these poems, sometimes in earlier versions, first appeared:

"Snake" and "Helictites" previously appeard in *Bucks County Writer;* "Karla Faye Tucker Says Goodbye to Her Body" (abbreviated form of "Karla Faye Tucker Who Was Executed . . .") and "If You Are Reading This" in *Cedar Hill Review;* "The She-Bat" and "Goat Island" in *Chiron Review;* "Last Plaster" and "The Span-Worm Moth" in *The Drexel Online Journal;* "The Book of Maples" and "The Trials of Love" in *Hanging Loose;* "News from the Big Bang" in *iris: a journal about women;* "A Misty Day on Mt. Nebo" in *Jewish Women's Literary Annual;* "Sundry Blessings" in *Kerem;* "Sandwiches and Dancing," "Bamboo," and "North" in *Loonfeather;* "A Jar of Roman Glass" in *The Lyric;* "The Honeymooners," "The Museum of Anthropology," "Nocturne Trying to Be a Love Poem," and "And Then" in *Mad Poets Review;* "Myrmidia" in *The Nebraska Review;* "The Death of the Milky Way" in *The North American Review;* "How to Do It" in *One Trick Pony;* "Ash" in *Paper Street;* "Beata Bonizzella da Trequanda" in *The Poetry Miscellany;* "As a Greek, He Used Honey" in *Poetry New York;* "Lullaby," and *"Vamos a Morir Juntos"* in *Schuylkill Valley Journal of the Arts;* "Miss Keller Returns to Her Senses" in *Yellow Silk II: International Erotic Stories and Poems.*

"The Honeymooners" received a Judge's Choice Award in the 2000 *Mad Poets Review* competition. "Nocturne Trying to Be a Love Poem" received Third Prize in the 2001 *Mad Poets Review* competition. "The Museum of Anthropology" and "And Then" received Judge's Choice Awards in the 2001 *Mad Poets Review* competition. "How to Do It," "Myrmidia," "And Then," and "News from the Big Bang" won the 2002 Robert Fraser Competition in Poetry.

"A Misty Day on Mt. Nebo" also appeared in the Israeli journal, *Helicon,* in Hebrew translation. "The Honeymooners" and "Bamboo" also appeared in the Albanian newspaper, *Rilindja Demokratike,* in Albanian translation.

Special thanks to Betty Rossi, Gail Rixen, Christopher Bursk, Richard Jackson, Betsy Sholl, Gerald Stern, Roger Weingarten, and David Wojahn for their advice about specific poems, their inspiration, and encouragement.

This book is for Steve, Lauren, and Benjamin.

"... up to that point I was pursued by the love of exactitude
which the majority of people mistake for truth."

Eugène Delacroix

TABLE OF CONTENTS

I

How to Do It

My heart was with the wild
raspberries because the blackberries
had fiercer thorns, less sugar,

and bigger skirts of poison ivy.
It was as if someone had left a window open.
My hair blew like curtains

as I stood before Mill Creek
where the raspberry canes looped like green garden hoses
or straw for an enormous basket.

Then I watched
a small snapping turtle swim beside his mother
until she submerged, as a mother will

when she seeks the cool depths.
I tossed raspberries into my mouth
as fast as I could pick them, thinking:

this must be how a bear lards up for winter
or how a pirate feels when he stuffs
beaded goblets into his sack.

Better than any pie these were,
but when I tasted spider web on one,
I knew I had been caught

in my greed. Moderation in all things,
sighed the wise. All the sweetness
you can seize, laughed the thief.

Stump

You could say it wore a skirt of ivy flounces—
still had that much self-respect,
hadn't realized it was dead yet, kept pumping
sap to the ghost of its branches

that rose like a glass dream. You could
call it a sort of Viennese table or a mess
after breakfast: spilled syrup
without the pancakes. Or that it was the sliced off

breast of a saint—a wound
with red ants quietly nursing, and
blow flies—those busy iridescent bruises—
swarming in like Hell's Angels

on a rumor of free beer. Or
that it was no longer
a plant at all, but the corpse
of an animal. You could offer

that the maple might have crushed
your roof in a storm or that you had to have the light
each morning the way a child needs a big glass
of milk. Or that it was the El Niño winter

that made everything crazy,
made February break into a fever
and the six-legged drunks wake up
five weeks early. You could say that the stump

was a bitter fountain or maybe
a wild barrel of hope spilling
its sweet water over the ivy frills and bark, and into
the dirt making a kind of dark batter, or

that it was glad to be drenched in its last
wet joy, as if green, or the love of green,
was what it lived by.

One of Those Days

As if it weren't enough today
to have a wide-eyed woman
attempt to convert me to butter

from margarine, I had a vision
of the wind barrel-jumping
runaway trashcans and tried

to chase after them
donning a rabbit suit
for extra speed but failed

even to snag a rotten carrot or
a lousy honorable mention. It was
one of those days between worlds,

the air clear as grappa. Small wonder
that trying to catch my breath I stumbled
into a cat's cradle a spider had strung

between the ornamental plums. I was like
a fool on fire rubbing
the pale protein from my skin, bursting

into my own kind of Tarantella
alone and without music
like the fly I smashed that morning

with a rolled-up newspaper. Who was he
to buzz at my window? To whirl his dervish
wings across this glass?

Blue Ape

Some of the 2% of me that is not chimpanzee
is sky blue. No one can see that part
when I play in the blue fields or swing

through the blue trees. I want to believe the moonlight
is my lullaby, but often the night
just keeps me up with its black coffee.

I suspect those jagged scraps
of light among the leaves
are perfidious stars that change

the definition of north and south
each time I beg directions.
Sometimes I travel on a false passport,

lie to get close to my companions, or
think my blood vessels are harp strings.
When the Minstrel God is giddy

from spinning on his tire,
he plucks ballads on them
until his fingers bleed.

Of all stringed instruments
the body's finest, and yet
it is the voice that convinces the red rose

that it is blue, charms the wild grape
from the forest. What is ultimate happiness?
I ask those comedians behind the dark screen.

The promise of greater happiness is such a terrible nag,
they laugh changing their fiery patterns.
Sometimes I try to find blue through my palm

as if it were a magnifying glass or a telescope,
and sometimes I take your hand in mine
if only for a little while.

And that makes me feel better—if only
for a little while. I try to temper the ape.
Thus, for a spell, I do not eat or make love,

and live unsociably with a single folding chair,
and am ashamed to be covered with skin.
An embarrassment to the prim God of Waistcoats

who shields his eyes in my presence
for my gleam can be murderous.
Perhaps the God of Bellows

blew his breath into me. Perhaps he regrets it
when he sees me walk a millimeter above
the glittering sidewalk, pondering happiness

and its many disguises. Sometimes I beat
the drum of my chest. Sometimes I touch
my heart with my blue knuckles,

confessing my uncertainty, my dullness
before you, Iron Goddess of Mercy,
who stirs a savage teaspoon of honey
into my white cup.

Maybe I am unable to recognize my joy.
Maybe I do not acknowledge my darkness.
What does the ape know of happiness?

A Jar of Roman Glass

How faithful it remains. This jar that first
cupped millet, barley, wheat in its pale green
palm and pleased the cook with its pearly sheen
of lavender and rose; that never burst
upon the marble floor; that, from its space
breath blown then tightly capped against the air
and spoilage, freely gave the cook her share
of grain and fed her; has ended a vase
that keeps her ashes. Now her flour sees
the other side of what is lovely. I
wonder: the pinks and purples, do they light
the inside, do they make her happy? A breeze
from somewhere ripples the green mineral sky.
It doesn't comfort me. I thought it might.

Beata Bonizzella da Trequanda

You could say that she was into leather.
Or that a woman of her years
should be a little more modest. Or that
it wasn't her fault the bishop
laid her in a glass coffin.
I think the dead are ashamed
because they know they are corrupt,
and only when they fall entirely
to pollen can it be said that
time's redeemed them.
As for Bonizzella,
no one knows how fast she lived,
how young she died—
only that she left a beautiful corpse.
Or so the winemaker's daughter testified
in 1500 when she found the pious maiden
in the church of Trequanda perfectly
fresh two hundred years
after her natural death.
Though she never made saint,
clearly she deserved to be
Blessed Patroness of the Well Preserved.

Now in May when the grapevines folk dance
arm in arm in their long green rows,
Bonizzella with her bony hooked nose
sleeps through her feast. She does not
hear the marching band
sigh its praise up and down the steep street,
nor see the carbon paper storm of swallows,
nor the thick-ankled village matrons
trudge in celebration
stiff in the dour suits they also wear to funerals.

How is it that they have clouds
for hair and faces the colorless tint
of Sodoma's transfigured Christ
whom I saw rising
in the chill and musty
church? For years I will call to mind
the three young women
with their long legs, copper-black hair,
who sipped chianti and laughed
in the sidewalk cafe opposite the church,
meaning no disrespect

only that they were not pilgrims
yet. I think it was the spring breeze
that moved them and which made me groom
my fear in the storefront window
and smell the potpourri of the church air,
the grief of the wild gardenia.
I thought of what is being taken from me
and will not be given back.
Taken by a serious mouth and deep eyes
so gently, so slowly
at first I did not notice.

Snake

There's the wag and where's the rest
of him? Quick
S of matterless
motion. Ever-changing signature.
Belt upon the floor without its shirt and pants.
O where is the hard evidence
of being? There is no fear like the fear of snakes

unless it is thrill, its white cousin.
The chance encounter
with a milky stocking caught on a log.
Is that the definition of ghost
or careless love—that slipping free
of all restriction, all consequence?
There is no thrill like the thrill of snakes

though for some their length
is a form of love.
Once I knew a boy who embraced their loopiness,
draped a green tree python
over his soft shoulder—
oxbow of a leather river,
long cool arm of a movie star,
sequined esophagus he stroked
and never found its clinginess too much.
The python? It couldn't get enough
of the boy's 98.6 and nuzzled his neck
with its wise triangular head.
There is no love like the love of the unloved

unless it is escape.
Consider the liquidity of the snake,
the unstoppable timeline of its form,

how a thin one pours
through your grip like toothpaste.
In a pet store a corn snake
slid like a lost friend
from the hole between my finger and thumb
and would not come back to my fist—
inch after inch
of you-can't-keep-me.
There is no flight like the flight of snakes,

and it is not only that they slither,
constrict, sometimes inject the cruel
hypodermic of death.
If, as I do, you fear them,
consider the happiness of seeing
a snake's skeleton,
of warming your hands
over the pale radiator of its back
or dancing so fast upon its trainless tracks
you grow wings. It's that
or the unbearable vigilance of living.

Helictites

Drop by drop it grows its fangs.
Little by little it eats its black insides.
It fills its emptiness
(a century or three for every inch),
and it has plenty of time for this violence.
For a cave,
to build's to choke and die,
and yet that is so much better
than to dry and cease to shape.

But what strange forms this self-destruction takes.
Down here random pillars grow,
caryatids with their accidental drapes,
flowstone fountains,
calcite statues by the thousands—
until the place looks like
the garden of a robber baron.
The cave simply does not know
when to stop building.

Along the walls, the space bristles at its fate.
There the pale helictites
wave in the weatherless air.
How they grow—
not down from the ceiling
but out from the weeping walls—
and none longer than an inch or two.
You could say they are the hair of the cave,
or its worms, its cilia.
Or its prisoners, their fingers twisting
and reaching through the grate,
begging bread and mercy.
Or the speechless and the deaf,
signing to me: hurry, hurry.

Foot

No hand in this world, but a foot
that's always wanted to be a hand,
that's always wanted
to catch the falling,
heal the sick,
free the enslaved,
keep faith with those who sleep

in the dust. That foot in the world,
half blown off by what it sowed,
I have seen that it presses blood from grapes,
flattens the tulips
upon the long cry of its road.

That foot, the mad and the lovesick
think they see it.
They believe
it walks with them.
They believe it dances
for some fine reason.

Sometimes you want to dress
that foot in velvet or
bathe it, rub it with lotion,
bring it to your lips and kiss,
speak into it like a telephone
with words human and passionate.

The Kingfisher

Imagine how this time
he dressed to go out
choosing white turtleneck, blue vest,
blue blazer, vainly
trying to tame his overgrown haircut.

Perched on a maple
as a regular might steady his elbow on a bar,
he feigns laid-back,
but inside his puffed up little chest
he's obsessed
with dive! snatch! Even
dozing he dreams
of the minnows
like so many fingers
beckoning.

Suddenly
he beats
his wings into a hover,
plunges,
snaps a pale flickering
in his needle beak. Then
fast-slow-fast-slow
like a new driver
who can't
quite coordinate
clutch and stick shift,
the kingfisher flies
minnow to maple
letting the swimmer know

the passage out
of water into suffering,

that quick lift up
to the borderless,
unbreatheable, dry. By degrees
the kingfisher flips the thrashing fish
so that its scales will slide
smooth down the gullet.

Perhaps the minnow considers
what it would be like
to fall from such a height: if
there would be much pain
or release from suffering,
if to wriggle free would be a sort of victory,
a way of disappointing the tormentor.
And how strange

it would be for the child with the coffee can
who keeps trying to scoop me out
of my world into his silver trap
to find me streamside
on the grass. Would he scratch
his head in wonder?
Would he suspect it was the kingfisher
who raptured me?

Myrmidia

It is a small miracle that we do not fall
through their designs into the cold water
for they always seem to be ice fishing
at our feet or perforating the dirt
on their glorious chocolate ramble.
Considering their love of strategy,
it is strange that I have never heard
a single ant express worry
about where his next idea will come from
or fret over his inability
to focus. We read in their tiny
type so many lessons in virtue. Nor does
an ant cry out that his world has come
to an end because his brothers have died
in war with another colony or in a shower
of insecticide. Industry in spite of sorrow!
Wondrous lift on that silent black galaxy
of fellowship and self-abnegation.
O life of elemental purpose. O unexamined life.
Pulled like so many iron filings
to whatever is sweet or dead.

The Death of the Milky Way

What comfort is it
to be staring at a half-dead
plum tree and fireflies that spread

their nervous galaxy about the dusk,
holding hands with you after watching
astronomers on TV around a table discuss

the end of the world? For I
am greedy for twice, maybe thirteen times,
my lucky life

which in the last few years has begun
to swell almost to bursting. The thought
of such loss fills me with wanting, grief—

they say the end won't be disaster. Five
billion years from now
there will not

be a hot apocalypse, nor
judgment or crash,
but a lengthy sigh, while the milky

river of stars slowly
spills into Andromeda, each
happily surrendering

its name, boundaries, all
sense of what it was. So much space
gapes in each, the stars

will mix and not collide
as the glowing bodies mesh
between the cold dark sheets
of the void.

Bridge and Dover

With a little dust
                at the corner
of Bridge and Dover,
                    with a few dead leaves,
with the wind chasing
                 its tail, yapping
every third round or so,
                    I stepped into the whirlpool.
I think I wanted to prove
                  to the wind that I could
stand my ground and not
               be turned into
a daiquiri. I wanted
            to be the stick
and not the swizzle.
             An obelisk, a flagpole,
the number one—
          what we were all supposed
to look out for,
          the supreme ruler.

Gradually a too-heaviness
                 in the gut—
call it nausea, call it
              self-disgust
took over. What came up
              was a wide desire,
to be the circle.
           This was a great relief.
You can imagine
         the feeling of lightness
that came over me. I
           resolved to float above the gravel
like a trick lasso,
         to hover like a hula-hoop
around no-waist, to
          be what Mrs. Phelps with her pointy

bra called the place
                              holder. You could say I was
a Mayan, so endless
                          was my love of zero
 and frightening.
                      Does not the infant
cry for her swaddling?
                          Does not the shut-in become
one with his bed and chair?

It was not that I wanted to vanish
                                      exactly but to be an O
of air, turning expectantly,
                              always open to the next
rapturous displacement, ever
                                  opting to meet a new
danger with a big smile
                          and a Hello-My-Name-Is sticker.
Being blocked was what I
                          feared. Fulfillment I saw
as a kind of death,
                      a collapse of all cavities.
I thanked something
                      or other, maybe my parents,
for making me so
                      cleverly: a sieve of sorts
or a tea ball
              filled with holes that let
the void flow
              in and out. Made me hollow
at the core so
                that salads, love, and jealousy
could make their
                    circuitous journeys.

Forget what you've heard.
                          Nature adores a vacuum.

If not for nothing
                    into what would molecules
diffuse? Into what
                    would the universe
cast its particles?
                    Where would the road go, or
my memories, or that
                    thought in the gray trenchcoat?

I am saying grace over all kinds
                    of emptiness:
thanking all the architects who
                    never built anything,
the lovers who never made love.

                    I stroke the paper
spine of my *Selected Rilke* and
                    thank Rainer for transforming
so much into the pure intensity
                    of something or other.
Most of all I thank Col. Fred Cherry,
                    the former prisoner of war,
who no longer hated
                    his captors and even returned
to Hanoi to visit them.
                    Exile the all-too-solid
citizen of yourself,
                    said the shot-down pilot.
I took a deep breath and
                    spun like that faint eddy of dust
at the intersection. I did
                    a little ballet, though
I only knew one step.
                    I went widdershins,
I nearly disappeared,
                    but somehow I found a fence post
and caught myself.

And Then

On that day the passenger pigeon
will return. Your sunburn will decide
not to become cancer. You'll remember
where you left your wallet, and it will
be there undisturbed. You'll forget
your lover told you to hang yourself
with the telephone cord. Your neighbor
with the loud radio will sell her house.
You will know which papers to keep
and which to throw out. You'll find the friend
you seek at break of day. Thereafter
you will be known by another name.

II

The Trials of Love

You should know what Helen Keller knew,
that *the fearful are caught*
as often as the bold, and absolutely
no one can save you. Still, you try your luck
with the Chinese placemat
that advises the dog not to nip
at the claws of the dragon, admonishes the snake
not to slither about the hooves
of the boar. Beyond that,
security may be pure superstition.
Observe the signs—
pickpockets are working the weekend
bread and vegetable market,
there's rat poison beneath the box
hedge. Be good and kind, but remember
just being alive may be
a high crime—even the innocent
die for it. But don't
let that depress you. If you feel
your heart is full of rue, rejoice
that your nose isn't stuffed
with wormwood. Be fashion forward—
wear pearls before the grand
jurors, red nail polish when lowering
your right hand to the
Good Book. Know that apples
are full of juicy wisdom
and cyanide-laced seeds,
that the cops really do want to
trap you speeding, but
contest the ticket:
they respect that. If you're guilty,
read Dante and find
that to be caught in clashing
winds is bad, worse

to be buried in ice up to your double
chin where others are likely to trip
on your head especially if
you're a bosom friend with a wire
secreted within the folds of your person.
Know that in the court
of infatuation, all of us
should have immunity. That if you don't wash

your clothes others will test them for DNA.
Prepare for the day your doorbell rings
and a special prosecutor asks
if you are now or ever have been
mad with desire, demands
you list the names of all
the people you've ever loved who,
in turn, will be subpoenaed and pressed.
On and on it will go until
everyone is implicated and charged
with excess.

Last Plaster

(Scrovegni Chapel, Padua)

Before heaven and hell soaked
into the wet plaster,
I saw the dead climbing
out of their bathtubs to be judged,
the saved reaching up
like a forest of golden spoons
through the cloud pudding.
How their facial muscles
must tire from so much smiling,
their arms ache from that eternal stretch
of praise.
Despite their just desserts, I believe
the good are starved

for attention. Hell's where all
we tourists congregate.
It's more down to earth here:
the fresco so brown and asquirm
with the naked it's as if Giotto
went digging in the garden and uncovered worms
or opened the curtains on an operating theater

before painkillers. I wince
in amazement. What did that man do to be hanged
by his genitals? Peering through her binoculars
a traveler asks, Why is that woman being flogged
by a moldy devil? Why is that man suspended
by his tongue?

Who are the wicked?

And is real hell this merciless
or is Giotto exposing Scrovegni justice,
a medieval muckraker sneaking into the prison,
then quickly painting his report?
As if brush and color could halt anything.
Besides, who'd believe something this monstrous
could happen
down the street from the chestnut orchard
and the flute maker's?

Aiming at the Germans
dug in deep in Padua
the Allies hit the church next door
but missed this chapel by mere meters.

Thus the young woman
with the long luxurious hair
and the shapely backside continues
to be flayed
and no one saves her.

The Widow Who Met Her Lover on a Rooftop

Encircled by the fighters in the thick dust,
she stood, said the *Times*, breast-high in a pit:
her head a better target for the cleric
who pitched first. How not to think of Jesus
saying, "Let him who is without sin cast
the first stone"? Then the righteous and bearded hit
her square on the nose, chipped her teeth, split
her lip. But she was hard headed. She lasted
longer than her lover. Her skull was so tough
the faithful had to walk up and drop boulders
on her to finish her off. Such are the forces
of the fiercely passionate when they crush
Love's rebels. In bed that night the soldiers
embraced their wives. They were cold as corpses.

In Kandahar, Afghanistan, the Taliban's Ministry for the Promotion of
Virtue and the Prevention of Vice condemned a widow named Nurbibi
and her lover, Turyalai, to death by stoning for adultery. This stoning,
one of several ordered by the Taliban, took place in August of 1996. The
facts of this case were reported by John F. Burns in *The New York Times*,
November 3, 1996.

News from the Big Bang

Because they believed that sex with a virgin
would cure their AIDS, many men sought out
young Laxmi Krishna in Brothel 64
even though a girl cannot be a virgin over and over.

This is why it matters so much
that Dr. Williger and his team in Chile
have found the biggest star cluster in the visible world.
After three billion years it is still sending
its ridiculous brilliance in every direction

even to Tsering Lama who protested,
"I only made 30,000 rupees—$500.
And I didn't sell her. I rented her out."
Every day 20 or so Nepali girls
are stolen or lured from their villages,
then sold as sex slaves in India
where prostitution is legal but only
if women choose the life, are paid, can quit
when they want to. So it is in our star-

pocked world where the Great Domain,
the Mass of All Known Masses, blazes
with its 11 galaxies and 18 quasars.
Did you know that a quasar can shine with the light
of a trillion suns? And that loved ones sometimes

put photos of lost girls on the Internet?
Laxmi wanted to go to school. Her stepmother
refused. So the fourteen-year-old took the bus to Katmandu
where Mrs. Waiba promised her a job
but sold her
instead of jeans to Tsering Lama.

So it is in the morning paper.
So it is on this blue and green dot
which may be the only place
where there is help and safety.
That is a lonely thought, and who knows if Laxmi Krishna
thinks it when, unable to sleep, she looks up

at the stars that sprinkle their pure lights
over the aching body into which so many men
have died.
Nothing you can touch
in this world is real for very long.
Maybe that's what she thinks
when her heart does not flare with rage.

O New Delhi police who rescued Laxmi
as she escaped one night with a girlfriend
from Brothel 64, who sent them

to Maiti Nepal, the woman's shelter. O Inspector D. B. Rai
who arrested Tsering Lama
and brought him to the dying girl.

O Laxmi facing your tormentor,
slapping him with your rubber sandal,
screaming in your tiny voice,
"What have you done to me?
How could you take away my life?"

O quasars that shine like a trillion suns.
O light from The Great Domain that hasn't stopped
piercing the universe. What should I say to all of you?

Bamboo

Glueing my teeth together with Milk Duds
at the old Tivoli
so that I could not even gasp—
I watched the emperor's lackeys
set a peasant over a patch of young
bamboo. A few frames later
he was shishkebab.

Imagine grass doing that—
limp bland shoots you
eat in stir fry stiffening
to a squad of killers.
Should I be grateful that the new culms,
which can spike up 16 inches in a day,

call a halt to themselves at 65 feet?
Maybe it's their way of saying
there is a point beyond which
terror can be no more
terrifying, pain no more
painful. But enough of optimism.

It will prevail,
cockroach of the plants.
After Hiroshima, bamboo was the first
green thing to reach out of the ash,
and now residing in its calm
clump on Gravel Hill Road

you'd hardly know it had a history.
It putters around in its garden,
struggles to love those it must live with,
waves its green fringe to whatever
has run away with the wind.

Goat Island

Amid the loosestrife
which was the same purple as her dress,
she pressed her hands together
and prayed for something over
the river that curtained down
the rock shelves frothing, so
blue slate and turbulent white it seemed
an X-ray of sheer menace. We

are leaving,
said the praying woman's husband. Fearful
of being abandoned on Goat Island
yet knowing her meditations might not
have the effect if rushed,
she nevertheless hurried her prayers, turned
her back on the river, cast a coin
into the fury. I looked at my own husband
staring at something on his shoe
and I said,
God of the lucky penny and loosestrife,
of the purple dress and
of the great unleashed,
God with His hands tied, God who has
no-man, no-woman things to do,
one day against
my dry logic I will also
ask something of You.

Karla Faye Tucker Who Was Executed in Texas by Lethal Injection for the Pickax Murders of Jerry Dean and Deborah Thornton

I
Says Goodbye to Her Body

This is the last time I take
a shower. But why
should I rub away
any more of myself—
my cells, my stink, my oils? Until
now I never realized
that the body anoints itself. I

should be tender to my hair. It
used to be so tangled and so
wild—I think of all the years
I wrestled with it.

This is the last
time I shit. Why have I never
before seen that
as the little death it is?

This is the last time I touch
my breasts.
What a strange thing a body is
tipped in its own pleasure.
And I wonder
if pleasure is the end of flesh
or if the end of flesh is pleasure.

I drink a cup of tea,
warm in my palm like another hand.
If only
it would hold me. This

is the first time I see my own face—
looking back from the glass
in these mortal doors. What
a funny thing it is, a face,
a round thing with holes
that let in the world.
A holy thing, I smile
the last time I smile.

II
Mother Love

Maybe Karla had been stoned from 10 till 24
and maybe her mama taught her
how to sell herself when she was just 14,
gave her drugs the way other moms gave
clothes. Maybe Karla loved her mother,
had to punish Jerry Dean
because he stabbed a hole in her dead mom's picture.
Who can say why Karla came
every time she picked him
or why she turned the ax
on the white shape of his woman?

Maybe it was Jimmy Leibrant, the rat,
who saved her,
or the cops who brought her in,
or the Bible she stole from the county jail,
or Jesus or Pat Robertson.
Maybe jail became her church.
In Mountain View she did come
to see the big picture.
Who knows? Maybe
she was just grateful
to get off drugs and men,
simply live
where she came to love the Lord

and the company of women. Maybe
the death penalty's just another crime.
Or, as the 700 Clubbers say,
she should live because she was born again.
And maybe we should render unto Texas
that which is Texas'.

Karla said that when she goes home
somewhere high over Houston
she'll be so busy!
Many folks have asked her
to deliver messages to their dear ones.
Said she was sure that if you're poor,
a sinner, homeless, lost in the dark,
the Lord wants you that much more.
Said she loves us, will see us all
when we get there. So
Texas gave her its justice, and
where is my love and where is my mercy?

And why is my heart so hard?
Why is my neck so stiff? Maybe
it was the way I slept on it
the evening that Karla lay down on that gurney
and offered her arm to the grim technician.
She said, plucking at her skin,
"This is not who we are.
We are much more
beautiful than this."

III

The Book of Maples

If as some scholars suggest the entire Book
of Maples unscrolls
like so many small fists,
there will be so much luck in the trees
that I will have to hire the palmist,
Mme. Theodora, to interpret all the lifelines
for me. Holding those little green
hands in her wise ones
she will decode their cuneiform,
foretell my future in pure
Sumerian, accepting my idiosyncracies and
credit card. As a bonus she'll give me
the best recipe for spiced wine with
honey, it's hard to know who to trust
these days. Even though I've been told it's bad
practice to reveal my hand,
every so often I do it anyway
hoping to be a little less nervous,
a little less lonely. My doctor
told me to take a little white pill
once a day for anxiety, but a pastry chef
said I should fold my fretfulness
into lemon scones, eat them
with raspberry jam, sweet butter, and coffee.
With someone very dear to me.
By a picture window
framed by white curtains
through which we can see a stream
bending beneath the green clouds
of the willows, bending so many times
it won't let us see
very far into the distance.

Ash

Ablink with the yellow leaves of the ash
the eye-blue almost loved the motes
more than the clarity. Each tree flaring
like a struck match,
and all around me
the leaves spinning and tumbling
like the skins of those who cannot stop falling
in love, in their blue sheets
tossing and turning. Say they were like the gold
shower of Zeus coming to Danae,
or the quick lights of self-
immolating rocks screaming
through the thick invisible,
or like that money my mother said
didn't grow on trees—
a blizzard of yellow
bank checks all made payable to the foolish,
the lucky, the desirous,
the you and me,
those who never knew how to spend their wealth
or could never spend it wisely.
Then on the rich
green grass
there passed the shadow
of a turkey vulture. It was
like pure darkness projected up
from the lower.
Overhead like a cinder or
a lone pilot orbiting, and it eyed me
with the cold black bullet of its eye
from where I stood
in the bright trees.
You have too much, you want too much,
you take too much, it muttered.
And though I was no brave woman,
out of the blue I blurted,
It was never enough. Never enough.

Miss Keller Returns to Her Senses

The voice of her left and right
hands cried out, *Carmine! Amber!*
India Blue! upon the wide
stretch of his chest. *Peter Fagan,*

you are my lighthouse, she spelled
deftly across the little bridge
of his cock. On her palm
into which he normally pressed
news of the Great War or Chautauqua

business, he nested dozens
of kisses, then sunk
his teeth into the soft

mound of her eloquent thumb. *Helen,*
my rose and thorn, his fingers
confessed to the inside

of her arm. On the nape of her neck
he scrawled, *Swear you are mine.* His fingertips
were fierce with her breasts
which could suddenly hear
nor was her dark eye

blind. Then like the strikers
on the picket line, her fingers traveled
down the length of his spine
to the small shallow where

she tapped, *I will always be separate*
even from you, translator
of the world to my flesh—
this is my crime. She gasped

as he signed and deeper
signed; then without hesitating
she guided him into the darkness.

Sandwiches and Dancing

That was what the sign said,
and we were hungry for both.
You tried to look in the window.
In the sunlight, it was
nothing but a mirror. Merciless
the way it reflected us.
Heavens, we looked love-starved!
Our clothes so loose they
were practically falling off,

and the glare so strong
you had to cup your eyes
to see inside. No one
was dancing, but sure enough
they were eating sandwiches
and they were laughing.

So we ordered, too.
Two $5 lunch specials:
tuna and Yankee pot roast with horseradish
sauce on nice Italian buns.
And it came with a cup of soup
and chips. It was delicious,
but there was no dancing!

Later you put your hand on the table
as if to your coffee cup,
but it was my breast you touched.
And I asked you if your hand was
happy, and you said it was
ecstatic, it was laughing.
It had a sandwich and
now it was dancing.

If You Are Reading This

GIRL WITH DOG IN RAIN! Sweetheart, where are you now?
Saw you at 16th and Walnut with your chocolate lab under an awning.
It was raining parking lights and car horns. I was the guy double-
parked delivering a tray of bagels to a corporate meeting. Nice stuff, 5
flavors, cream cheese with chives, butter daisies. Our eyes met, do you
remember? I can't get you out of my mind. [Box 347]

OLD LADY AT QUIK MART. When I weighed your peppers, you
said I had my thumb on the scale, then you called over the manager
who yelled at me and docked my pay. You: Old bag in tan overcoat,
muffler, purple pocketbook, evil eye. Me: Goatee, geek glasses, facial
hardware. Please give me the opportunity to stab you. [Box 1601]

CHAD, LET ME EXPLAIN. That guy you saw me with on the R7
local on Columbus Day meant nothing to me. He's just a commuter.
Your silent treatment is unbearable. I'm beggin' you baby, come back!
[Box 776]

PENN CENTER ELEVATORS FROM 16TH TO 30TH FLOOR. I
want to push your magic buttons. I want to draw Mona Lisas on your
beautiful skin. You: Backless red dress, black heels. Me: Bald guy, 35.
We rode up together, you got off at 19. I was too shy to talk to you.
Now full of regrets. How about sushi or tantric sex? [Box 1446]

GUY ON R7 LOCAL OCT. 10, EVENING COMMUTE. You sat
next to me and suddenly it was Valentine's Day. You liked my Offspring
button. I told you about med tech school. You let me take your pulse. It
was almost like holding hands. You: Hilfiger sweatshirt, laptop, got off
at Somerton. Me: Hip chick, red hair, capri jeans. Let's pick up where
we left off. [Box 777]

YO! YOU THERE ON DEERPATH DR. I'm the telemarketer you dissed. Wasn't selling you anything, SOB, just giving you a free estimate on kitchen cabinets. I know your number and where you live. Call now to apologize. [Box 961]

OFFICEMAX, FEASTERVILLE, YEAR AND A HALF AGO. You: long black trench coat with three-piece suit. Me: Asian girl with black jacket, wet curly hair, tight black pants, sunglasses on my head. You stared at me a long time waiting at checkout. We looked at each other as you walked out. Will renew until I find you. [Box 1674]

Ace Bar

Ever wonder why the girl with the laptop
doesn't mind having her boyfriend
put his hand up her shirt
in Tompkins Square Park or why
the man with the snake tattoo is
writing his love a billet doux
at Ace Bar, why the pit
bull isn't fighting but the sheep
dog is and why the scaffold tree
at Avenue B and 7th Street is hung
with a blue stuffed rabbit, a plastic
ice cream truck and other
junk that's lasted
longer than its joy
or why no one picks the daffodils
and the scallions even though someone
left the gates of the garden
open and why today of all days the pigeons
flutter in the voice of Rinaldo
as he begs the bright air for his beloved?

Céret

Their stucco walls staggering
up the slope drunk on the local sweet wine
or sober but doubling over
from some mysterious dyspepsia, possibly
dragging themselves up the town's bleached
stone stairs like half-melted
penitents beaten
to a fever by the unforgiving heat,
the homes of Céret were dying
to share their secrets.
Fanning in five anguished greens
the ferns at their feet squirmed in a wormy
impasto. Ready to splatter
on the red roof tiles at any moment,
the bilious cumuli of trees
threw no shadow. Odd
the houses were still intact and
that people still lived in them
though life was shaky, yet as long
as the doors revealed
only their numbers,
crops could be harvested and sold
at market. But because a dark-eyed
troubadour told them
that confession was good for the soul,
the villagers thought if they exposed
everything their pain would go away.
Every day from 1920 to 1921, the town begged
Soutine to cut it open
as if he were a surgeon
or a ritual butcher and not
one who loved
to layer hemorrhage red and
purulent yellow thickly over a martyred horse
and assorted roosters, who was a brother

to the soul silently shrieking in the dead
animal. Eventually, though,
he obliged Céret with his palette knife.
As he cared more about the innocent flesh
and less about their cruelties
and suffering,
he let the townfolk confess
off-canvas. They blurted. They purged.
Soutine had to wear ear plugs as he painted
what was not so much a town anymore as a thorax,
the stucco walls now white ribs
striping the hillside, terracotta
shards fallen into intercostal meat,
central stairs now spiky
vertebrae, and if green
could be driven mad, that was the color
of the self-hating vegetation.
In his spattered smock he stood back—
the townfolk looking over his shoulder
at the painting which at any moment
could have spilled off the canvas—
and he asked Céret:
Now are you relieved?
Now do you feel better?

Nocturne Trying to Be a Love Poem

In this life
there is so much more to talk about
than you and me. With far more starlight

do I trade secrets with the arbor vitae
that sways spitelessly in the breeze.
At most my hand speaks

to what is blameless—
the small of your back, soft
skin over triceps.

Yet sleep *is* conversation.
What some say sex is—
a turning together, our bodies

whispering fitfully of the time
they will no longer have each other—
death, divorce, whatever breaks

the habit of marriage.
Look at me! One never dependent
on nicotine or alcohol.

Sleeping together.
We still do that—
as if trying to make friends

with the enemy,
as the elderly do
who nap in the afternoon.

We sleep and our souls rise
off our backs as if they were high
on laughing gas. In their pale pajamas

they rock and roll to the Top 40,
happy as two amnesiacs
who forgot they broke up, until

they remember they are astronauts
who can't come back. Blithe
and brave no more, they tear

at their velcro, fog their visors
over the terra firma they miss so much,
the earth's glamorous blue gaze.

Happy as a . . .

Are they really happy or just blissed out
from suffering fools? I think they keep quarts
of secrets—their own, the cod's, the shark's—
and smile at all they know but don't let out.
And this is odd, for the clam's all mouth:
two calcified lips that will not talk,
as sociable as rocks, each shy heart
locked whose deep mystery is power
and loneliness, whose safety is salty joy,
whose dignity's worth dirt. They need
to be taken from the sea and boiled
alive or steamed like stubborn envelopes
before they sweetly, tongue to tongue, confess
the unhinged life has always been their weakness.

As a Greek, He Used Honey

How is it that you have but one body,
one heart, one cock,
and yet can love so many women—
faithless to all, yet loyal
to each with your tongue and your honey—
your single mouth singing
so many songs of lust and tenderness?

Now you are in a mad rush for joining,
in the present lateness wanting
not less but more.
And you say you feel guilty. Ha!
Ask us if we care!
It is we who will be the death of you,
your jealous maenads who love you to pieces.

At your funeral we will all be there,
wild with grief, each
with a toe or a finger and bit of your heart.
And we will wave with our bloody hands
to your head and your lyre
and your dear mouth still singing
as it floats down the river
we filled with our weeping.

The Span-Worm Moth

I'm in a throwing-out mode, you confessed
while I watched a span-worm moth struggle
in a spider web by the baseboard.
August. In the third-floor study
I could have killed for air conditioning and
anything and tonic. Feeling guilty,
I let the wings beat in the sticky threads.
Into the heap, you said tossing
Thomas Moore's *Care of the Soul*, which
first sounded like an embalming
manual or a how-to you might want to read
while waiting in your open coffin
for the relatives to arrive, but
which was, in fact, *A Guide for Cultivating Depth
and Sacredness in Everyday Life.*
As if existence
were not pointless. Or maybe
Moore suspected it was and so had to invent
a reason for it. The next day I learned it
was a New York Public Library
Book of the Century and heartily recommended
for holiday reading by *The Book Lover's
Calendar*, though I doubt I will ever savor
it while leaning on a pillow next to you.
So many smart people write so many
smart books so few will ever read
or remember, you lamented gleefully in your fever,
which I caught. I tossed four collections of poems
over your shoulder. You pays your money
and you takes your chances, you crowed.
Then I freed the moth,
and we threw off all our clothes.

Lullaby

From an Estonian folksong, with thanks to Jaan Kaplinski

I was the worm in your liver, the fish
in your stomach, the bird
in your bones.
I drank your blood, breathed your air,
ate the vessels of your heart,
said harsh things with your tongue.
When I left you, you chased after me crying,
You are my life!

A Misty Day on Mt. Nebo

Not that it was a cake walk,
but the way we tell the story the best
part of the journey wasn't our rediscovery
of milk and honey, but
the chase through the split
sea and trek through the red
kiln, the wandering and straying
from faith, the habit of playing
fast and loose with destruction. Together
twenty years. Even if we

are married for forty I don't
think we could ever set foot
in that historically certified
dreamhouse we promised
each other. Besides, my nerves just couldn't
take so much happiness. Though
in a deli once,
having a pastrami on rye with a slice
of pickle, I dreamed
of it. In Jordan in the parched

Mountains of Moab we stood
hand in hand that August on the top
of Mt. Nebo in backpacks and hiking boots,
our canteens brimming with sweet water
from Wadi Musa—that place in the wilderness
where Moses, breaking faith with the Lord
and furious with the tribes, struck
the rock twice bringing water
forth and his own sad end,
having come that far
only to be forbidden

the promised land.
In that heat I considered what Heraclitus said,
that personality is fate. How,

as with Moses, anger and impetuosity
also run in our veins as does
the tendency to break
tablets, faith, engagements, doors,
and how that puts so much distance
between us
and the longed-for world.
From the summit of Nebo
I gazed over the distant bliss—
forgetting for a moment the dung
of the sheep that give the milk,
the buzz of the bees
about the honey. Khaled, our

Palestinian guide, led us up
so that we could look out like Moses
over the land, but
there was a mist. All
I could make out was the black snake
of the Jordan, the fringe of Jericho,
the Salt Sea that shone like a lead
mirror in the air that exerted
so much pressure. Somewhere in the haze
hid the city, which just
for that moment I believed
was a place of peace. Then I wondered

what if the Absent-Minded One, Blessed be He,
had accidentally scheduled
a misty day to show Moses
all that he suffered for, but which
could never be his.
So I just imagined the haven, which,
if you were of a mystical turn, you might
call my personal Jerusalem—bright
purpose each morning, ecstasy
each night, endless
patience with the children, rich
dark coffee with steamed

milk, a little plate of
sesame candy made with honey, peace
in the house, courage,
work, friends, and this
I wish, my love, with you beside me
in the wilderness.

Vamos a Morir Juntos

To see the two I had to squint
into the mirror
the artist stuck to the half-opened lid
of their silk-lined matrimonial
coffin. That made their side by side
deliciousness multiplied,
and me the voyeur who stared
at the matchstick groom and cornhusk bride.
I'm still struggling to understand
the Mexican romance with death.

What is it like to love
someone so much you'd rather die
together than let death
part you? Unbearable for one
to go on as four loose ends
of a love knot or as a bug
on its back with nothing to hug
or hump but the thin air.
In widowhood imagine combing
all the lost and founds
of the world for another
with whom you have so much
incompleteness in common.

As for these sweethearts,
I suspect them of deeply passionate
fights, Carta Blanca bottles shattered
on the floor; threats, truths plunged.
Oh, killing love.
Love that is a shard in the heart.
Remorse that bleeds
in big white spurts of glue.
I couldn't shake those lovers from their box
or separate one without tearing the other.
Who loves like this? I asked the mirror.

Elderberries

Where are the elderberries of my school age,
the buckeyes? My red velvet cap
with the fake brown braids? I cried through
three kleenexes searching for it
up and down Warder. And these names
fading in my address book.
Bob Knapp and Julie Ivins who didn't mind
my joining them in the Baths
of Caracalla. And Mary Crutcher who ran the city desk,
leveled with me about pouting
in the office, taught me the pyramid style,
never revealed her sources.
Where is Nanette Berger—so wise about men,
so unlucky in love, so prone to run off
to Palenque every six months?
And Laura Braddy, who never criticized
my torn sneakers, showed me how to rent
a room by the week at Shirley Hall,
and when the girls moved out in June
I got their plush towels, Balenciaga, and caviar
from the dumpster.
But I moved away and you can't keep all your friends
forever. Whatever happened to nervous Nancy Moon
who never put nutmeg on turbot,
Marla who only ate popcorn, or Gwen
who wouldn't speak to me because
I was white but was always nice to Pam Shu?
Or Dan Driscoll who said I would never
go far in politics
because I wanted to be liked too much?

And Lynn Levin, for whom is her name
written on the wind with a moving finger,
past whom does it drift like a twig
down the great muddy? Does Donna Greenstein ever
wonder about the copywriter who used to sing
cowboy songs from the next cubicle?
Or Mal—does he ever sigh
with relief that he has never seen
me again? And who was that guy
with dark brown hair whose name I can't recall
who took me to Angelo's for barbeque?
The lost ones can't help it, they open
their pale mouths from the thick green walls
to which they are safely chained and blow
their sweet breath, small darts.
They are that powerful.

The Museum of Anthropology

The Eskimos did it on occasion, and
it might seem all right to eat
a person when times are tough
but unthinkable to dine on flesh for pleasure.

It might seem all right to eat
your enemy—a way to polish off your fear.
But *unthinkable* to dine on flesh for pleasure?
Consider your lover's palm. Like sugar to a horse.

Your enemy: to eat him is to polish off your fear
and know him inside out.
Consider your lover's palm. Like sugar to a horse
whose large lips fumble as they reach.

To be known inside and out
may be a deeper thing than love
whose large lips fumble as they reach
the bitterness they take for sweet.

The Honeymooners

It is as if they are walking under parasols
or should I say paralunes?
that neither is burnt in the quick light.
They stroll past us eating vanilla ice cream,
and their snowy pleasure is so simple,
so milky sweet.
But for us what tempts is more complex.
Consider the taste of this orange you feed me—
tart and honeyed, a little bitter,
bringing a burst of heat to my forehead,
the aromatic oil sharp in my nose
like the pleasant sting of Eros.
And the pulp a sticky handful of jewels,
topaz or maybe citrine,
the peeled skin on the floor
aglow like a city
seen at night from an airplane,
on fire with what is orange, manmade,
and through the dark deep endlessly attracting.
If only this were a harvest moon,
but it is white.
Its bony light limes what it touches.
Its lye ever so patiently works through our flesh,
but what tender love we make in our corruption.

The She-Bat

Bats did not live in the eaves,
you said, nor did bumblebees though
three attended her in death. We
found her like a crumpled

glove, brown leather, on the step
before your study door as if
she had been knocking there
a very long time.

I wonder how long the ardent
thing had banged about the attic,
alone, craving
the lidless evening—the bat

without her mate, without a bite
to eat (I do not think
she had a taste for bees).
After how much high-pitched calling out

and how much awkward singing
did she fall before the door?
I think she knew it was a door.
That is what terrifies and grieves me.

9:27 A. M.

Wasn't this the weather you loved
to walk through, the morning chill retracted
like the claws of a cat
napping between the window skirts,
the vapor of its tail curling

before the backfire of pigeons?
Didn't 9:27 spark like a nightclub,
bright with the brassy sax
of traffic, the red back-up
beeps of a bread truck pulsing

through it all the sad hearthrobs
of your miserable school days begging
you to mambo? Wasn't this the city
you loved to walk through, the columbarium
of the old mill staring

at you through its punched-out
lenses, a parade
of sway-backed mules lifting the tired
lineworkers into a snowy forest?

Didn't a cop bark
his warning as the sun stropped
the sidewalk causing the pigeons
to rise and the bread

in the bakery? All across the sky
there were shelves of clouds
and their sorrow reached down
like a white stick

to trace you. Very often
you think of your lost
friend Connie, her long hair billowing
like the black gown

of a justice, floating
up to your table for coffee at the Pink Rose,
her mouth kissing

the mismatched china. Her gaze was
the color of postmarks, her words
punctured tires.

Wasn't this a morning that loved you
the way you wanted to be loved? The air
like an ivory pillow, every car
singing to you from its fading

radio. Weren't you supposed to be
sweeping the floor with the claws
of pigeons as their hearts cried
out? It is a curse to be wanted.

North

To see an Arctic swan above the frozen lake,
to feel its *oohooh* auger a hole

into your heart is to know you should not love
your unhappiness, although that is easy to do.

To hear the wind sough through the birches
and pines as if the woods were a raw harp

playing every possible note at once—
is to hear a splendid sort of emptiness,

the way white is the concentration of all color.
Now I remember what it was like to wake

from a faint, feeling light and displaced.
It was like staying overnight at the home

of a happy couple who prepared venison and wild rice
for dinner, who kept a *bas relief* of naked lovers

on the ledge of their enormous bathtub.
I walked on a ridge above the marsh

and saw that I did not have to change my life,
that I could go on perfectly well as I was:

gaveling the air for justice, forcing my heart
toward mercy, bending before all branches

so as to walk humbly: for I have heard
this is all that is required of me.

I heard the grouse beat the air. I saw
the trees the beaver gnawed as much out of love

as fear of its long teeth. I had this sharp
vision before the leaves masked the North

in green disguise, and I was of two minds:
one of them was sighing.

Sundry Blessings

On awaiting an important phone call, an invitation, or other good news

Blessed are You, O Lord, who allows me to live in the brief world of the possible.

On seeing a person who has one foot on the ground and is trying to put the other down

Blessed are You, O Lord, who causes the earth to fall away from a man's step.

On having someone see in your work something deeper than what you intended

Blessed are You, O Lord, who has not made me my only interpreter.

On being rejected by a school, an employer, or by voters

Blessed are You, O Lord, who has not required me to change my life.

On hearing of a massacre, a comet strike, or a family burned in a house fire

Blessed are You, O Lord, who has created forces beyond Your control.

On standing before a tree that bends with fruit

Blessed are You, O Lord, who causes happiness to weigh heavily upon me.

On seeing a fledgling drop from a crow's mouth

Blessed are You, O Lord, who surprises from a great height.

On being unable to sleep

Blessed are You, O Lord, who gives the night legs.

On arising

Blessed are You, O Lord, who has given me another opportunity to show courage.

On not being recognized

Blessed are You, O Lord, who has given me another face.

Photograph by David Graham

About the Author

Lynn Levin was born in St. Louis, Missouri. She was graduated from Northwestern University and received an MFA in Writing from Vermont College. Her poems and translations have appeared widely in magazines throughout the country. Bucks County, Pennsylvania, Poet Laureate for 1999, Lynn Levin is also the winner of the 2002 Robert Fraser Competition in Poetry. She teaches at Drexel University. Her first collection of poems, *A Few Questions About Paradise,* was published by Loonfeather Press in 2000.